Front Cover: Reina del Mar at Liverpool Landing Stage, 1956
Back Cover: Construction of the Metropolitan Cathedral, 1966

© 1993
 The Bluecoat Press
Bluecoat Chambers
School Lane
Liverpool L1 3BX

Typesetting: Typebase, Liverpool
Origination: Creation Graphics, Birkenhead
Printed by: GZ Printek, Bilbao

ISBN 1 872568 04 1

LOOKING BACK

Liverpool and New Brighton photographed by Elsam, Mann and Cooper

Text by Colin Wilkinson

The Bluecoat Press

LOOKING BACK

The name Stewart Bale meant nothing to Leslie Cooper back in 1930. An eighteen year old in search of work, he was prepared to try anything that offered prospects of an interesting career. When a girl he knew mentioned there was a photographer's apprenticeship going at her firm, he thought it was worth applying for, although he had no experience or knowledge of photography. To his surprise, he was offered the post, on a month's trial, at a commencing wage of 10/- a week and, so, began a five year apprenticeship.

Stewart Bale were commercial photographers. Edward Stewart Bale, the founder, originally owned a thriving advertising practice but, finding it difficult to commission photography of a high enough standard to meet his clients' needs, he decided to employ his own photographer. As a result, Frank Elsam was taken on and, soon afterwards, Bob Mann as his apprentice.

Bale soon established a reputation for quality and the company grew so rapidly that, by the time Leslie Cooper joined, the advertising side had virtually disappeared. Based in the Bear's Paw Building, on Lord Street, Bale had begun to corner the market for shipping and architectural photography previously monopolised by the London firm of Bedford Lemere. Operating out of Liverpool actually worked in Bale's favour, for Cunard and other main shipping companies were based in the city and had no hesitation in switching their allegiances from Lemere.

When Leslie started, the basic working tool was a 12x10 plate camera. With the exception of Bedford Lemere, few other companies used such large negatives, preferring the lighter and less cumbersome half-plate cameras. The large glass negatives produced exceptional results but they were heavy and expensive. In a good day, it was possible to take up to sixteen plates a day. No duplicate photographs were taken; Bale expected 100% accuracy and got it.

The level of craftsmanship required ensured that Leslie obtained a unique apprenticeship. In other aspects, working life could be difficult. No personal transport was available and photographers would strap their equipment to the front of trams when out on assignment. There were bonuses for a young man, however, as the job often involved travelling around the country, particularly to photograph

ship construction. Leslie regularly photographed both the *Queen Mary* and *Queen Elizabeth* being built in Glasgow. During the course of a week, perhaps a hundred plates would be taken of every aspect of the ship; from details of the engines to interiors of passenger lounges. The large interiors presented a considerable technical challenge because of the relatively primitive lighting available and the limitations of the glass negatives. To overcome such problems, long exposure times were essential, with each section of the interior being individually lit or 'painted with light'. Now, fast films and sophisticated lighting technology have removed many of these technical problems, often to the detriment of the final composition. When each shot takes over an hour, discipline is essential to make sure every aspect is correct, unlike today's commercial photographer, who run off rolls of film in the expectation that some of the exposures will be satisfactory.

Leslie continued working with Bale throughout the 1930's. The clients represented a roll-call of the great Liverpool firms; amongst them Frisby Dyke Department Store, Heaton Tabb (ship furnishers), Alfred Holt Line, White Star, and Lee's Tapestry Works. Memorable assignments included the construction of the Mersey Tunnel and the Anglican Cathedral. Work for the Admiralty was sometimes less enjoyable and, in 1939, involved photographing the submarine *Thetis* after its tragic accident. When War broke out, Bale laid off most of the staff but, in 1946, work resumed as normal.

Stewart Bale had built up a company widely regarded as the best commercial photographers in the country. When he died, his son Ted took control and continued to maintain the high standards (although neither he nor his father were involved in the practical aspects of photography. Ted, himself, died of illness during the War and his widow, Hilda, took over the management. Leslie felt the changes were beginning to effect the quality of the company's work but was happily employed until a dispute over wages. At the time, he was paid £7 a week but the London rate was 10/- more. Along with senior photographers Frank Elsam and Bob Mann and a number of more junior staff, Leslie was prepared to resign if the demand was not met. Surprisingly, the junior staff accepted the existing wage but Frank, Bob and Leslie decided to hand in their notices.

So, in 1946, Elsam, Mann and Cooper bought a Morris 8 car, took offices in 14, Dale Street and commenced trading in their own names. Leslie was not particularly close to either Elsam or Mann, being many years their junior, but the new company arrangement suited

Liverpool Docks, c.1935
One of Leslie Cooper's first photographs for Stewart Bale. He remembers asking the train driver to let off steam to heighten the dramatic effect of the photograph.

him and he was immediately immersed in the challenge of getting the business off the ground.

Fortunately, the partnership managed to take some of Bale's clients with them. In particular, Turner's Asbestos Cement helped them through the first year. Before long, they had English Electric, Meccano, Cammell Laird and Blackpool Tower on their books and the company prospered. Frank Elsam was the main photographer, with Leslie taking charge of the darkroom. Bob Mann was a retoucher and finishers, whose painstaking skills included the ability to write perfect captions on negatives in mirror writing.

The company expanded and, in 1958, moved from Dale Street to 6, Princes Road. The wide diversity of work included architectural, advertising, industrial and public relation assignments. No wedding or social photography was undertaken. The client list included virtually all the many major firm in Merseyside and, as the reputation of Stewart Bale declined, Elsam, Mann and Cooper became the leading local company.

The photographs chosen in this book are a small sample of the kind of work undertaken. Starting with post-war scenes of bomb-damage, they document the physical and social changes over the following decades. The Overhead Railway, Shakespeare Theatre, liners at the Landing Stage, crowds at New Brighton and workers at Meccano are all memories of a lost era. The novelty of television in a nurses' home, GI's at the Grafton and the crowds waiting for the Isle of Man ferry are here, frozen in time by a photographer whose main concern was carrying out his client's brief.

Frank Elsam died in the late 1960's and Bob Mann a few years later. Leslie Cooper is in his eightieth year and is somewhat bemused by the interest his photographs create. Photography to him was a job he enjoyed and he was skilled at. Security problems in Princes Road forced him to transfer the business to Fenwick Street, in 1989, but the move did not work out. Early in 1991, Leslie decided to call it a day and take a rest after sixty years in photography. Fortunately, his negatives have survived and the selection in this book are testimony of a remarkable career.

Acknowledgements

The prints reproduced here are used with the kind permission of Leslie Cooper, Oxton Studios and Roger Quayle Photography.

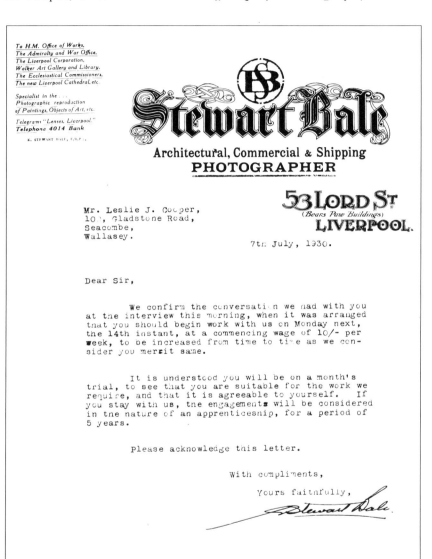

Leslie Cooper's letter from Stewart Bale confirming an offer of a photographic apprenticeship.

The photographs of Elsam, Mann and Cooper

War Damage, Derby Square and South Castle Street, 1947

St George's Place, 1957

Liverpool Overhead Railway, 1956

The Last Days of the Overhead Railway, 1958

The Empire Theatre, 1947

Mersey Tunnel Entrance

Bunney's (Corner of Whitechapel and Church Street), 1956

Church of Our Lady and St Nicholas, 1956

New Shakespeare Theatre, 1957

The Grafton Ballroom, 1949

Meccano, Binns Road, 1950

Liverpool Wash-house, 1956

Washerwomen, Liverpool, 1952

Washerwoman, 1952

Cammell Laird, 1957

Leaving Work, English Electric, East Lancs Road, 1950

Sports Shop, Liverpool

Blake's Car Showroom, Hardman Street

Christmas Concert, English Electric

Nurses' Home, Liverpool

The Twist, 1963

Celebration, Liverpool, 1949

Waiting for the Isle of Man Ferry, 1948

Passengers for Britannic Arrive at Riverside Station

Boarding a Liner at Liverpool Landing Stage, 1951

Reina del Mar at the Landing Stage, 1956

Ferry Crossing, 1947

Elmgarth, 1960

Mersey dredger, 1958

Liverpool Waterfront from Woodside, 1954

Launch of Windsor Castle, *1959*

38

Launch of Cheshire, Cammell Laird, 1956

Runcorn Transporter Bridge, 1962

New Brighton Pier and Shore, 1948

New Brighton Funfair from the Tower Ballroom, 1948

Tower Ballroom, 1949

New Brighton Pier, 1951

Funfair and Promenade, 1949

Pier Concert, 1961

Chairlift and Funfair, 1961